Awarding Greatness

Nobel · Caldecott · Pulitzer

Alison Auch

PACIFIC
LEARNING

© 2004 **Pacific Learning**
© 2004 Written by **Alison Auch**
Edited by **Rebecca McEwen**
Designed by **Anna-Maria Crum**
Photography courtesy of The Nobel Foundation (cover, pp. 6, 8, 9, 11, 12, 13, 14, 15, 17, 18); The Randolph Caldecott Society UK/www.randolphcaldecott.org.uk (pp. 21, 22, 23, 25, 26, 27, 28, 29 [both], 30, 31, 33 [illustration]).
Additional photography: Scott Bauer/ARS/USDA (pp. 4, 46); Ian Waldie/Getty Images (p. 5); Hulton Archive/Getty Images (cover [Randolph Caldecott], pp. 20, 34,); Anna-Maria Crum (p. 33 [medal]); Library of Congress (pp. 36, 38, 40, 42, 43); FPG/Getty Images (p. 39); Fox Photos/Getty Images (p. 41); Spencer Platt Newspapers (p. 44).

08 07 06 05 04
10 9 8 7 6 5 4 3 2 1

Published by
Pacific Learning
P.O. Box 2723
Huntington Beach, CA 92647-0723
www.pacificlearning.com

ISBN: 1-59055-417-5
PL-7512

Printed in China.

Contents

Introduction

Every year, people all over the world make outstanding contributions to art and literature, conduct groundbreaking research, and do remarkable and inspiring **humanitarian** work.

These achievements can help shape the way we see and understand our world – or even save lives. A journalist may report a story that uncovers illegal government activities. A doctor may

develop a new kind of treatment for a devastating disease. A novelist may write a book that changes people's lives.

Sometimes, these gifted and dedicated artists, writers, and researchers receive special recognition for their work. Some win awards that have been created to celebrate their accomplishments.

Some of the most well-known awards today include the Nobel Prize, the Caldecott Medal, and the Pulitzer Prize. Each of these awards is named for a man who did exceptional and innovative work during his lifetime. Each of these men has a remarkable story.

CHAPTER

Alfred Nobel and the Nobel Prize

The day was bleak, and seven-year-old Alfred Nobel was at his home near Stockholm, Sweden. He was stuck in bed – again – while his older brothers were at school.

Alfred's mother, Andrietta, sat beside her son's bed. Tears ran down her face as she wondered how much longer Alfred would live.

▶◆◀

Alfred Bernhard Nobel was born on October 21, 1833. He was terribly ill as a young boy, and most people – even Alfred himself – felt he wouldn't survive to adulthood.

Yet amazingly, by the time he was eight, Alfred grew healthier and was strong enough to begin first grade. He was a bright child, and he caught up to his grade level in no time.

Alfred's father, Immanuel, was living in Russia to make equipment for the army. When Alfred was nine, he and his mother and brothers went to join Immanuel there.

The laboratory where the Nobel family worked

Immanuel soon noticed Alfred's intelligence, and he believed that his son showed great promise as an inventor. When he turned seventeen, Alfred's father sent him abroad to see the world, and to learn as much as possible.

When he returned to Russia, young Alfred joined his father and brothers working in their engineering company.

During his travels, Alfred had learned a great deal about something called **nitroglycerin**.

He took what he had learned, and he and his family conducted experiments on nitroglycerin. They had to be extremely careful, though, because the stuff was highly **combustible**. Still, Alfred was fascinated by it – he was sure he could turn it into an explosive.

Because nitroglycerin was so dangerous to work with, Alfred had to find a safe way to use it before he could put the deadly liquid to a more practical use.

Eventually, he came up with a new explosive that used both nitroglycerin and gunpowder. He called it Nobel's Patent Detonator.

Young Alfred

There were still problems, though...
big problems. Although Alfred could
now use nitroglycerin as an explosive, it
continued to be dangerous to transport
and store.

Alfred was driven. Even after a
nitroglycerin explosion killed his
younger brother, Alfred continued his
work. He was determined to make the
stuff safe and useful.

Alfred was experimenting with a new
substance called *kieselguhr*, which was a
chalky packing material. He mixed it
with nitroglycerin. He tried his best to
make the mixture explode, but without
igniting it, he couldn't. He shaped it
into sticks with his hands. "This is
incredible!" cried the excited inventor.
"I have finally found a way to safely
harness the power of nitroglycerin!"

Alfred called his invention dynamite,
based on the Greek word for power,

"dynamis." In 1867, he patented his remarkable new explosive.

Engineers blasting a tunnel with dynamite

Alfred Nobel's new dynamite literally changed the entire world. Engineers used it to blast the tunnel that runs under the Alps. Huge rocks were removed from New York Harbor using the powerful explosive. Geologists used dynamite to uncover incredible mineral deposits under the Earth's surface. It was used in weapons. People even used dynamite to try to make rain!

By 1873, dynamite had made Alfred a wealthy man, and the inventor bought a mansion in Paris. There, he continued working and inventing, for he was never without ideas.

As Alfred grew older, it seems that his conscience began to trouble him. His major inventions – dynamite and more advanced explosives such as gelignite – were being used to make weapons, yet he said he was against war.

Villa Nobel

Over the years, Alfred had become friends with an Austrian woman named Bertha von Suttner, who was a peace **activist**. In the letters he used to write to her, he expressed

Bertha von Suttner

his hopes that the sheer horror that new weapons added to combat would actually help end it.

In one letter, he said, "…on the day that two army corps can mutually **annihilate** each other in a second, all civilized nations will surely recoil with horror and disband their troops." It seemed his feelings on war were clear.

However much Alfred wrote against war, though, late in his life he became actively involved in developing weapons. In 1894, he went so far as to purchase a factory that made weapons.

Alfred Nobel

At the same time, he was still contributing money to his friend Bertha's peace organization.

It may be impossible to know for sure what this brilliant man felt and believed, but it is sure that peace was on his mind.

14

In 1895, Alfred finally came up with a way to balance his work and his desire for peace. He wrote his final will. Then, once his plan was set, he could get back to work.

In the last years of his life, Alfred spent a great deal of time working at his weapons factory, even though his health was deteriorating.

Alfred's will

Then, in 1896, he grew very ill, and on December 10, Alfred Nobel was dead.

After his death, it was discovered that Alfred's will specified that the bulk of his money must be used to set up a fund for five separate awards.

Each year, the prizes were to be awarded to people who had done work that had contributed to the good of humankind. The prizes were in physics, chemistry, medicine, literature, and peace. In the late 1960s, an additional award for economics work was added.

People around the world were confused and stunned. How could a man who had contributed so much to modern warfare be concerned with peace? Why did he choose literature and science? What about medicine?

Alfred Nobel had always been a private, often lonely, person – he probably didn't reveal many of his inner thoughts to most people. However, he made sure that after he was gone, the world would have a much better picture of his passions and beliefs. In doing so, he has encouraged and rewarded some of the world's greatest thinkers.

>+<

Each winter, the Nobel Committees consider the nominees for the different awards. They make recommendations to different organizations, which make the final decisions. The process is a long one, and it isn't until the fall of that year that the organizations finally select the Nobel Prize winners.

The winners must be picked by November 15, and the Nobel Prizes are presented on December 10, the date of Alfred Nobel's death.

The first winners of the Nobel Prize

In Sweden, the awards for physics, chemistry, medicine, literature, and economics are presented by the king. The Nobel Peace Prize is presented in Norway. Winners receive a diploma, a medal, and a certificate stating the amount of money they have been awarded.

A modern Nobel Prize ceremony

The Nobel Prizes may just be the best-known awards in the world. Many people believe that, of all awards, a Nobel Prize is the highest honor of all for its recipient.

Trying to decide each year's winners takes much time and care. Every year, candidates for the Nobel Prizes are nominated to the Nobel Committee. A person might be nominated by Nobel **laureates**, scholars, or other qualified people who believe the nominee has done outstanding work. Because a nominee can be from any country in the world, the Nobel Prizes reach far and wide to make the world a better place.

CHAPTER

Randolph Caldecott and the Caldecott Medal

The forest was the only place that felt like home. There, the young boy could sketch plants and animals and make wood carvings. His father – a stern and severe man – was not there to try to push him into more serious pursuits. It was the only escape he had from the dreariness of his life, which felt so sad following his mother's death.

Randolph's childhood home

><+<

Randolph Caldecott was born on March 22, 1846, in Chester, England. As a little boy, he got sick with rheumatic fever, a disease that permanently damaged his heart. For the rest of his life, he was never very well and would tire easily.

That didn't stop Randolph Caldecott.

Fortunately, Randolph was a bright student so school helped him cope with his health problems, as well as his problems at home. Yet, probably more than anything, he found his truest happiness when he was drawing.

Randolph's father regularly tried to get his son to think in a more businesslike way. He insisted that Randolph work in his tailor shop. The shop was always sweltering hot, and Randolph hated it.

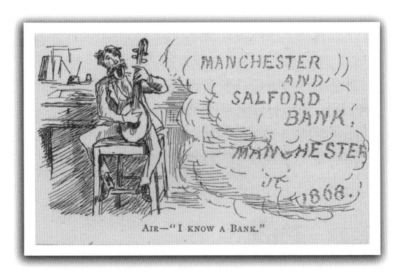

An early Randolph Caldecott sketch

To survive the work, Randolph would fade away into daydreams of his beloved woods, where he quietly sketched any animals that were around him. His father was forever losing patience with him.

Still, Randolph drew constantly. He never seemed to tire of it. It was hard to argue with that kind of passion.

Luckily, when he was at school, Randolph did find support for his art. The headmaster himself, Mr. Harris, encouraged the boy, and even managed to convince John Randolph to let his son take art lessons.

Many people believe that this Caldecott illustration is a self-portrait of Randolph as a young boy.

When fifteen-year-old Randolph finished his studies and had soaked up everything he could in his art lessons, his father found him a job as a bank clerk in a nearby town.

Randolph was good at his job, but he had a weakness. He drew all over everything! He even got in trouble with his manager for it. Randolph was a likable person with a "charming disposition," though, and in the end, his job was safe.

Then, in November 1861, Randolph's life changed. He had been home visiting his family when a local building burned down in a horrific fire. At first, Randolph had watched, shocked. Then he began furiously sketching the scene on his pad.

He decided to submit his drawing of the event to the *Illustrated London News*, which published it in December.

Randolph's first published picture, printed in the "Illustrated London News," 1861

Randolph became a local celebrity. Even his father was impressed!

Itching for more opportunities to make his living as an artist, Randolph moved to Manchester, England, when he was almost twenty-one years old. He still worked at a bank, but life in Manchester was more exciting and full of opportunities – very different from anything he'd ever known.

Eventually, Randolph joined the Brasenose Club, an artists' organization in Manchester, and his world opened up.

At the club, Randolph met many other artists and was able to make some great friends. He was more inspired than ever to make his art a full-time occupation.

Inspired by what he had found in Manchester, Randolph moved to London in 1872. He was ready to devote himself to art – even if it meant going hungry.

One of Randolph's newspaper illustrations

The London art world welcomed Randolph with open arms. Soon, he met a well-known artist named Sir Edward J. Poynter and began taking classes from him. He met many other artists and worked illustrating newspaper stories. His life was full and his schedule demanding.

Yet, despite the fact that Randolph truly felt at home in London, things were far from perfect.

Randolph's home in London

Randolph's work was exhausting him. His friend, Henry Blackburn, editor of *The London Society*, suggested that Randolph start illustrating books. That way, he could avoid the stress of the newspapers' daily deadlines.

Randolph jumped at the idea. It was a great time to be involved in book publishing. More people could read during the 1870s than ever before, and more people were buying books. Business was booming.

Soon, he was helping create a new and exciting series of books for children. Known as the Picture Books, they were published from 1878 to 1885.

There was something new about the way that Randolph illustrated children's books. His pictures were full of life, sometimes funny, sometimes dark and sad. More importantly, his

Randolph illustrating a children's book

illustrations didn't just support what the words said, they helped tell the story.

Children adored the books, and the series was a huge success. After years of struggling – and of battling poor health – Randolph was finally making a career with his art.

Look closely at this detail of a cat from one of his illustrations. Can you see Randolph's face?

In 1880, Randolph married Marian Brind. Randolph was blissfully happy. Marian soon became worried about her husband, though, who was sick and weary. So, in 1885, the two went to the United States, where Randolph could relax as he traveled and sketched.

Randolph would never return to his home in London.

The Ronde, a country dance

Marian Brind Caldecott is the woman on the right

As he traveled, the artist's health grew increasingly worse, and on February 13, 1886, Randolph Caldecott died in St. Augustine, Florida, at the age of thirty-nine.

Randolph Caldecott overcame many obstacles in his life to follow his dream of becoming an artist: a lifelong battle with illness, a father reluctant to support his passion, and pursuing a career in a field in which it can be tough to succeed.

Randolph was determined to make his dream come true, though – and he did. As an artist in general, but especially for his contribution to children's books, he was a pioneer.

►◆◄

In 1937, the American Library
Association (ALA) decided to create an
award for children's book illustrators.

Wanting to name the award after a
groundbreaking children's book
illustrator, the ALA chose Randolph
Caldecott. The first Caldecott Medal
was awarded in 1938.

Each year, anyone can nominate a
children's picture book for the
Caldecott Medal simply by sending the
book to the Association for Library
Service to Children – a section of the
ALA – by the end of the year.

To be nominated, the book's
illustrations must be a main part of the
children's story and help to tell it.
Nominated illustrators have to live in
the United States. Plus, the books have
to be published in the United States.

A special committee reviews the candidates. Finally, one Caldecott Medal winner is chosen, along with a small group of Caldecott Honor Book winners.

In the spring, each winner receives a medal that shows two of Randolph Caldecott's illustrations.

The Caldecott Medal is not only one of the highest honors a children's book illustrator can receive, it also stands as a tribute to the amazing Randolph Caldecott.

The medal design is based on one of Randolph's illustrations

CHAPTER

3

Joseph Pulitzer and the Pulitzer Prize

Eighteen-year-old Joseph Pulitzer stood by the edge of the ship. It was nearing Boston, Massachusetts, and he had to make his decision. "It's now or never," he thought to himself. He swung his legs over the deck railing, closed his eyes, and jumped ship.

The young man sank under the frigid water. As he surfaced, he gasped for air. The water was cold. No, it was freezing! There was only one option now, though – he had to swim to shore.

►◄►◄

On April 10, 1847, Joseph Pulitzer was born in Mako, Hungary. His father, Philip, was a successful grain dealer, and Joseph's family was wealthy.

In 1853, things changed for Joseph. That year, after moving his family to Budapest, Joseph's father died. Not long after, Joseph's mother remarried. Joseph loved his mother very much, but he despised his stepfather.

When Joseph was only seventeen, he left home to join the Austrian army.

Rejected by the army because of his terrible eyesight, Joseph eventually wound up on a boat to the United States to fight in the Civil War as a Union soldier. It was on this 1864 voyage that he jumped overboard so he could collect his own **bounty**, instead of leaving it to the recruiting agents that were paid to find people to fight in the war.

Serving as a foreigner in the U.S. Army wasn't easy for Joseph. He had backbone, though – and plenty of intelligence – so he wasn't going to let anyone stand in his way.

Emancipation Ordinance, 1865

After the Civil War ended, Joseph headed to St. Louis, Missouri. In 1868, he was hired as a reporter for a German-language newspaper called the *Westliche Post.*

Joseph quickly built his reputation as a journalist. Soon, he began to expose **corruption** wherever he could.

The newspaper's owners were so thoroughly impressed by his dedication to uncovering and telling the truth, they offered him partial ownership in the paper.

Joseph couldn't believe it. For someone who was only twenty-five years old, it was a wonderful offer – one he couldn't refuse.

Joseph threw himself into his work, and loved it. Under his care, the paper's circulation grew. Then, after a candidate he supported for U.S. president lost, Joseph became depressed and sold his share of the paper.

Still, Joseph couldn't stay out of the newspaper business for long. Running newspapers was in his blood, and in 1878, he bought the failing *St. Louis Dispatch*. He rolled up his sleeves and got to work.

To save the paper, Joseph had to start selling more papers – fast. He also wanted to stay committed to causes, such as corruption, that were important to him. His goals would work well together.

Joseph continued to attack crimes

such as insurance fraud and gambling. To tempt readers to buy his paper, he also wrote flashy headlines and nasty articles about people's private lives.

Home of the "St. Louis Dispatch"

A famous story in the "St. Louis Post-Dispatch"

Some questioned why he was airing so much dirty laundry. Was he trying to sell papers no matter what, or was he committed to real issues? He was accused of **sensationalism**. Still, his paper sold like crazy.

In time, though, problems at the paper, which today is called the *Post-Dispatch*, erupted. Plus, Joseph's health, which had never been good, got worse. His eyesight was failing. Sales of the paper dropped.

"The World"
newspaper
print shop,
New York

In 1883, Joseph decided to travel around Europe for an extended rest, but first he made a stop in New York City – one that would change his life.

While visiting his brother, Albert, who was also a newspaper publisher, Joseph heard a rumor that a local paper called *The World* was for sale.

Suddenly, Joseph was the owner of another ailing paper. He set to work exposing government corruption, horrific living conditions in the city, and more. He also put in sensational stories about tragedy, gossip about the wealthy, and tales of bizarre crimes in *The World*.

Headlines were short, as were the articles.

Joseph's pioneering approach of mixing important issues such as reform and corruption with sensational "news" was a winner for him. His paper sold.

Meanwhile, Joseph's eyesight continued to fail. Soon, on doctor's orders, he gave up his position as editor of *The World*.

To make matters worse, he was also suffering from an illness that made him extremely sensitive to noise. He traveled the world searching for cures, but found none. Still, Joseph stayed involved with *The World*. He just could not give it up.

The Pulitzer Building, New York

In 1896, Joseph became involved in a huge battle with another New York newspaper publisher, William Randolph Hearst. They began printing sensational stories to grab readers from each other.

At one point, William stole Joseph's entire Sunday paper staff, including an artist who drew a cartoon called "The Yellow Kid" (named for the main character's yellow clothing). Joseph hired someone else to draw "The Yellow Kid." Now there were two "Yellow Kids"!

Later, the approach to journalism that Joseph and William both used to lure new readers and produce higher profits was called "yellow journalism."

William Randolph Hearst

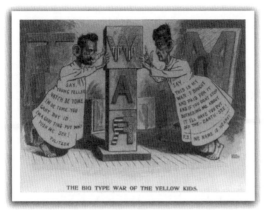

THE BIG TYPE WAR OF THE YELLOW KIDS.

An editorial cartoon about the battle between Joseph and William

Joseph eventually backed off from yellow journalism and again focused his attention on important causes.

Although he never gave up work, Joseph's health continued to get worse over the years. Finally, on October 29, 1911, the newsman died.

Joseph Pulitzer's work in the newspaper business has inspired mixed emotions in many people. Some appreciate the revolutionary way in which he made newspapers interesting and accessible. Others only remember him for his questionable plunge into the world of sensationalism and yellow journalism.

▶◀▶◀

Above all, Joseph Pulitzer may be best remembered for his will. In it, he left two million dollars, part of which was to set up the first school of journalism at Columbia University in New York City.

Another part of the money was to be used for creating the Pulitzer Prizes, which were to be given out by the new school of journalism.

Originally, Joseph wanted awards to be given in four categories: journalism,

The Columbia School of Journalism

letters (books) and drama, education, and traveling scholarships. The first prizes were awarded in 1917, and today, there are twenty-one awards, including for poetry and music.

Each year, after all the entries for the prizes are screened, the Pulitzer Prize Board meets in the spring to decide on the winners. A week later, winners are announced, and people gather to hear the exciting news.

Pulitzer Prize winners receive money and special certificates awarded by the president of Columbia University.

The prestige of winning a Pulitzer Prize is tremendous. For many winners, the cash award is a distant second to the recognition and respect they will get.

Even though not everyone agrees with decisions Joseph Pulitzer made during his career, his name has become a synonym for excellence.

Story Background

People are capable of accomplishing amazing things. Each day, women and men may spend hours in a lab, or at a computer, or at a drawing table – they may even put their lives on the line to do their jobs. They are all working to make the world a better place.

The Nobel Prize, the Caldecott Medal, and the Pulitzer Prize are three awards that have been created to honor people's extraordinary achievements.

Here are just a few well-known

winners of these important awards. Perhaps by receiving these awards, each winner has inspired others to do the best work they can.

Some Famous Award Winners

Nobel Prize
Literature/1993:
    Toni Morrison, author
Peace/1964:
    Martin Luther King, civil rights leader
Physics/1921:
    Albert Einstein, physicist

Caldecott Medal
1964: Maurice Sendak, *Where the Wild Things Are*
1986: Chris Van Allsburg, *The Polar Express*

Pulitzer Prize
Breaking News Photography/2001:
    Staff of *The New York Times*, photographic coverage of terror attacks on New York City
Music/1997: Wynton Marsalis, *Blood on the Fields*
Novel/1983: Alice Walker, *The Color Purple*

Index

Glossary

activist – someone who works actively for a cause he or she strongly believes in

annihilate – to complete destroy something

bounty – extra money paid when someone joins the military

combustible – when something can explode, often very easily

corruption – illegal activity, for example, in governments

emancipation – when people are freed from being under someone else's control. For example, the Emancipation Proclamation freed the slaves in the United States after the Civil War.

humanitarian – when a person does things that help other people

laureate – someone who has received an award

nitroglycerin – an explosive, poisonous liquid

sensationalism – news stories that appeal to people's vulgar tastes and that don't have much news value